# Prison Segmentation
# For
# Senior Prisoners

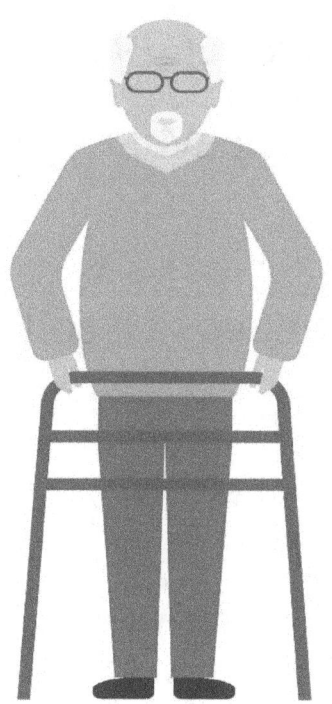

Reverend Mike Wanner

Copyright

October 29, 2017

Reverend Mike Wanner

Selected Images Used by License

# Table Of Contents

Table Of Contents ................................................................ 3
Introduction .......................................................................... 4
1 - I am Writing This Book Because ................................... 5
2 - Cost Of Keeping Seniors in Prison ................................ 7
3 - Disclaimer ....................................................................... 9
4 - Caution About Civil Liberties ...................................... 10
5 - Senior Prisoners Age .................................................... 11
6 - Wellness, Costs & Common Sense ............................. 12
7 - Collaboration Teams .................................................... 13
8 - Segmented Seniors Project Goals ............................... 14
9 - Request For Senior Segmentation .............................. 15
10 - Threat Assessment ..................................................... 16
11 - Medical Assessment ................................................... 17
12 - Diability Determination ............................................ 19
13 - The Complexity Of Change In Prison ...................... 20
14 - Self Aware and Nation Serving ................................. 22
15 - Angel Raphael Light .................................................. 24
16 - Thank You ................................................................... 26
17 - Don't Worry Ever ....................................................... 27
18 - Resource Books .......................................................... 28
19 - Angels Please Prayers ................................................ 30
20 - Private Channeling .................................................... 31
21 - Reverend Mike Wanner ............................................. 32

# Introduction

Some sources report that in America alone there are more than 2.3 million people in jail.

All the intellect in all those residents may not be used well because the owners of the brains are incarcerated, and a significant issue for them may well be their safety.

I, like most people, was oblivious to that fact until I was invited to look into it. I started channeling Angel Raphael in 2013 and began releasing little message sets as they came through.

In message set 16 of the Angel Raphael Speaks Series there was a message that has remained floating in my head since as topic for my writing.

The message I resisted was an invitation to visit jail energetically. Here is the content -

> "I asked Mike to Step into Prison Energetically
>
> I have asked Mike to get the address and location within a prison of a designated space so he can visit energetically and receive feedback for us to consider. Whether he will have time, interest or opportunity to do this will be interesting to see. As he writes this, he is not thrilled with the idea. We are already consuming a lot of his time." ARS16

# 1 - I am Writing This Book Because

I embraced the invitation in 2016. So far, The Angel Raphael prodding has had me publish the following books related to prisons:

1. Angel Raphael Speaks Volume 4: Angels, Addicts, Alcoholics & Prisoners - Oh Yeah!
2. Angel Raphael Speaks Volume 5: Prisoners Caring for Alcoholics - Australia In Miniature   Projects Intro
3. Angel Raphael Speaks Volume 6: Prisoners Caring for Addicts - Australia In Miniature For   Addicts
4. Prison Jobs Now: Providing Care For Addicts And Alcoholics
5. Angel Raphael Speaks - Prisons (A Kindle only book -2013)
6. Contained Care Communities: Concept
7. Australia In Miniature
8. Prison Possibilities Dialogue Series: Concept
9. Prison Possibilities Dialogue Series: Volume 2 Dialogues
10. Prison Possibilities Dialogue Series: Volume 3 Dialogues
11. Prison Possibilities Dialogue Series: Volume 4 Dialogues
12. Prison Possibilities Dialogue Series: Volume 5 Dialogues
13. Prison Possibilities Voluntary Exile: Concept
14. Prison Possibilities Correction Coaches: Concept
15. Prison Possibilities for Mexicans: Is A Boat Better than A Wall?
16. Prison Possibilities Family Time: A Reason to Thrive!
17. Prison Genius Pool: "So Much Genius In Jail."
18. Prison Possibilities Access Systems: Prisoner Access by Request
19. Prisoner's Lawyers Can Save The American Economy: Make A Buck Doing It & Be Thanked!
20. Prisoner Family Talks, Days, Stays & Vacations: Connecting Helps Healing
21. Prisoner Writing Projects: Write To Heal, Start Over & Reconnect
22. Prison Cell Clearing & Blessing: Clear Entities, Chase Ghosts, and & Create Sacred Space
23. Prisoner Professors: Show You Are Aware Create Change With Care
24. Prison Reiki? Maybe Someday? A Gateway To Help Heal Prisons & America?

25. *Judges and An Angel Rule On Possibilities: We Can Cut Sentences & Prison Costs*
26. *Ideas For Prison Wardens: Leadership Is Not Easy*
27. *Solitary Community: Could Community Support Cut Costs and Issues?*
28. *Prisoner Projects Communication Teams: Communications Can Change Lives*
30. *Motivating & Empowering Prisoners? Invite Prisoners To Find Their Motivation & Their Future*
31. *Prison Segmentation For Safety, And Sanity, Security, Peace, and Space*
32. *Prison Segmentation For Security*
33. *Dowsing for Prisoners; Answers from Above*
34. *Ex-Prisoner Possibilities With Real Estate Investors*
35. *Prison Segmentation For Joint Ventures*
36. *Prison Segmentation For Your Rehabilitation: R U Ready?*
37. *Prison Segmentation For Family Villages*

This book continues to carry the potential for rethinking that can help to reduce incarceration to those who we need to have there.

I want to trigger mindset shifts in the prisoners as well as employees and the community. We need a lot more Objective Productive Dialogues about Enhancing the lives of Prison Employees, Prisoners, Taxpayers and the Families of Each of these groups.

# 2 - Keeping Seniors in General Population

Segmentation offers the possibility to help senior prisoners in many ways. In general population, seniors can be more vulnerable than other adults.

Segmentation can help insulate seniors from younger prisoners. Aging seniors are also vulnerable because they may have less access to medical care than other free citizens in their region.

It is not exactly easy for their children to come check on them and give them moral support either. While the federal government in America has changed policy somewhat about keeping the ill in prison, that is not immediately transferable to the states and regional authorities.

There are a lot of different administrations that would need to evaluate the new recommendations and rule on their integration into the local system. While there is talk about Compassionate Release, there do not seem to be a lot of stories in the press of releases happening.

The possibility of compassionate release and probability is like many things in prison, complex. Citizens being safe from prisoners is so rooted in administrative mindsets that the system is risk-adverse. That position can be both understandable and justifiable but also economically dangerous for the nation.

The problem that stands out is that the American economy is failing because of continuing escalation of government expenses across the country. There is a critical need for common sense steps to mitigate the cost of incarceration and reverse the high number of incarcerated Americans when compared to other nations.

The land of the free has a lot of people who are not free. Please consider supporting some quality of life considerations.

Balance is essential for all things. The persistent question is whether the cost to the public of incarceration is in the balance with the value of safety it affords or is the collateral damage to families so intense that new ideas are needed.

# 3 - Disclaimer

I, the author, am not involved with prisons or prisoners but I have talked to many prisoners during Hospital Pastoral Visitations. I am sharing what is coming to me in an effort to spread understanding and trigger conversation that can be helpful. It may be that the discussion needs finessing and I invite your wisdom into the mix.

My guidance has suggested that a lot can be done. I will detail my views which are not the expert positions of a Corrections Officer or Corrections Administrator or Corrections Manager or Corrections Supervisor, or another expert who might be helpful here.

As I have said many times before, everything that I see about prisons seems to be so complicated. In the prison books, I suggest some things that have come to my awareness that align with channeled messages from Angel Raphael.

### Note

I feel that much can be done to enhance the success of prisoner rehabilitation when ideas are shared in a respectful way. I drafted a series of five books to invite submissions in a responsible format.

The message about the series can be found in the book *Prison Possibilities Dialogue Series: Concept* on Amazon or Kindle Link http://amzn.com/B06WLKSH77

The book invites further dialogues and collaboration which could help the whole system.

# 4 - Caution About Civil Liberties

The laws of America have standards that apply to Medical Care and privacy of personal information. It may be expedient to group prisoners by many factors so services and accommodation can be provided expediently and all efforts to do that must respect the privacy and liberties of each prisoner.

Program developments should include appropriate rights sensitivity, compliance and or waivers as may be deemed necessary by the counsel for all involved.

Proper documentation is not an impediment to upgrading service but merely an aid to prepare for appropriate process progress.

The best arrangement may be a participation agreement that is simple to understand but entirely inclusive of the benefits and the expectation for all participants.

Participation should be clearly optional and universally documented, and consideration could include a routine opt-out timeline that details the times and ways that a prisoner and or a prisoner's family get to reassess and or reset the criteria of participation.

Participation will be bilateral so that continuation of the arrangement must be bilateral in an ongoing relationship. Should either party decide to cease involvement, it must be done subject to the rules established at the outset of the agreement.

# 5 - Senior Prisoners Age

Life is fragile for us all and prisoners are as vulnerable to aging at least as much as the rest of the people of the world and perhaps more. Aging may be healthy and natural and progressive and subtle, but incarceration is direct and real.

The incarceration has interactions with many others and is probably nigh on impossible for outsiders to understand all the interactions that can impact on the peace of prisoners. While prisoners age in an environment that may be less than friendly, they may be motivated by conditions to accept segmentation that comes with reasonable expectations.

The safety of segmentation may be very welcome and able to allow possibilities that are not available in a general population. Each prisoner would have to decide for themselves.

Independent movement within a reasonable set of variable circumstances could have great appeal. Subject to the creativity of each prisoner in their use of space to make maximum advantage of all this can avail them of extraordinarily essential options.

Aging provides incremental deterioration and varies by each individual. Deterioration of capability and skills are a threat, and the new control and support provide community value.

Personal wellness is more likely in an interactive self-supporting segment of the facility than in a general population.

# 6 - Wellness, Costs & Common Sense

The safety increase via segmentation does not mitigate the actual costs of medical care that is needed but can avoid some expenses by merely controlling the vulnerability of seniors. The delivery of necessary care may be done in many ways, and the options can impact expediency, efficiency, quality, and ease.

Common sense can allow us to envision that convicted people can reach a point where they pose little to no threat to the community. When a critical level of disability limits the danger that a prisoner poses to the community, options can be considered to the complexity of medical care within a secured facility.

The American Civil Liberties Union (ACLU) has a lot to say about the incarceration of Seniors. Please visit their site at https://www.aclu.org and support their work.

I read there that –

"Elderly prisoners are the least dangerous group of people behind bars but the most expensive to incarcerate. "

## What Options Are There For America?

# 7 - Collaboration Teams

If a threat that existed is no longer dangerous, then how can we justify the expense of incarceration that continues to eat up the resources of the country? The answer to that question is in the comprehension of risks.

Reading the statement in the last paragraph on the ACLU website was a reliable indicator to me that we can begin to assemble a new assessment process. Segmentation could be the perfect greenhouse in which to grow a crop of freedom potential for prisoners.

It seems logical that deliberate planning and sensitivity to not tread on anyone's right could start a voluntary plan to change the setup for prisoners prudently.

The Steps that seem apparent are to:

1. Develop a Participation concept paper that details the project goals.

2. Develop an Application form for potential Candidates.

3. Invite constructive suggestions from the ACLU about the process that is being considered.

4. Await a response from the ACLU before publishing any proposals.

5. Offer to collaborate in an ongoing way with the ACLU to work on individual projects one at a time.

# 8 - Segmented Seniors Project Goals

Senior segmentation is offered as an optional program that can be applied for by prisoners who feel that they would do better without interaction with the general prison community. The intention is to efficiently better serve those who request it by providing them with some things that can ease their incarceration.

Segmented seniors will not be getting a country club experience but may be able to have some enhancements like:

1. Improved bathroom access

2. Less need to stand in a queue

3. Less need to interact with younger prisoners

4. More ability to be around prisoners who may understand their needs.

5. More ability to be around prisoners who may be in their age group.

6. More ability to be around prisoners who may be like a support team

# 9 - Request For Senior Segmentation

I would like to apply to enter Senior segmentation on a trial basis because of my age and circumstances.

I understand the program is optional and offered when space is available. I am willing to wait for a spot.

My request is necessary because

_____

_____

_____

_____

_____

_____

_____

_____

                                    Respectfully

                                _____

                                (Date)_____

# 10 - Threat Assessment

There will need to be an assessment of some kind about the threats that individuals pose to the occupants of the prison and external general communities.

Prisons can consider beginning to draft ideas that can be shared, assessed and developed. Restating the sensitivity to not tread on anyone's rights could start a comprehensive plan that can actually be launched as soon as philosophies are in harmony.

What can be robust but also appropriate? How can deliberate planning serve the prison and the prisoners?

Components that might help start the evaluation could be rooted in some digging into the details of prisoner propensities:

1. Violent History Episodes or None?

2. Provocateur or Self Defender?

3. Personal Growth or Stuck?

4. Cooperation Record?

5. Correction Officer Recommendations?

6. Occupants Perspective in Senior Segmentation?

7. Has Change or Rehabilitation Happened?

8. Have they Hardened or Softened?

# 11 - Medical Assessment

As everybody ages, their medical condition impacts every aspect of their life. The medical assessment would be necessary for the prison and the prisoner.

The medical assessment can contribute to and support the threat evaluation now and the foreseeable future. As this review is in progress, there could be a subtle but essential component that determines or at least considers the ability of the prison medical service to care for the needs of each prisoner from a complications perspective.

Medical services in a specialty facility can be much more available and much more economical to deliver. Full-service General and specialty hospitals have the economy of scale time efficiency and dollar economy advantages over a general clinic where everything has to be ordered individually and then delivered through security considerations and reviews.

Part of the due diligence could be a recommendation of a multi-level prognosis projection. This process could be projected as a monitoring schedule instead of a medical orders schedule so that the prison could not be criticized for delaying care that was ordered.

Patient medical condition changes can vary significantly by environmental impacts and living conditions. It may be fair to consider that deterioration could be slowed by changing the residence from general population to a segment that is more peaceful.

Stress reduction is an awesome improver of possibilities for anyone who needs to be at peace. I feel that so strongly that I have a whole website for stressed people at
http://www.StressReleaseCoach.com

There could be options for prisoners in between a prison clinic and a general or specialty hospital that could be efficient for the prison authority and beneficial for the prisoners. I do pastoral care at an inner-city hospital which treated prisoners in the general population for a long time but then had a lockdown prison ward for a while.

Eventually, they closed the ward and went back to guarded prisoners in the general sections of the hospital. It seems that efficiencies can change and prisoner care can change with them.

The answers for any individual facility could vary by circumstances and patient conditions. Efficiency and customized proper care can be very compatible.

Another option to consider could be a Contained Care Community like the book I wrote by that name.

# 12 - Disability Determination

Disability could be faked, but it could also be a cause for particular consideration if it is real and documentable. Impairment could be limited or absolute or progressive in a constant flux between the extremes.

Segmentation for seniors can by itself be a little easier to tolerate than the general population. Of course, I will repeat that in America alone there are about 6,000 lockups of one kind or another and each could be very different so my last sentence may be inaccurate where you are.

The reason for this whole book is to give seniors a little more space and a little more peace and a bit more consideration of their needs. I hope readers find it helpful but I also want to challenge senior prisoners to be on the lookout for others.

Shifting from self-interest to community interest could lighten the stress on the incarcerated tremendously. The shift will not come naturally when the personal program has been long set.

The security of segmentation can offer seniors a better ability to give what is needed to the many who did not get it in the general population. Giving and receiving can be concurrently beneficial when a peaceful present has helped one to get ready for the shift and then it is chosen.

# 13 - The Complexity Of Change In Prison

In chapter 2, I referenced the complexity of change in prison, and the tendency of the authorities to prioritize community safety without regard to the dollar costs. Nevertheless, we as a society need to be diligent in the spending of the limited resources that the taxpayers have paid.

To be considered diligent stewards of community funds, administrators can break down the process into a system that measures things more incrementally and determines what is working and what is not. Management is not easy, but it determines the quality of the lives for all.

Throughout my books, I talk about deliberately less confrontational paths instead of the traditional way that the prison system is changed. I believe that a baby steps process can be a very stabilizing influence on the broader community.

The little steps can involve many more contributions from staff who know the prisoners better than anyone else. Please understand that these suggestions are possible acceleration tracks that might be possible for exit candidates of quality.

Nothing included here is intended to displace any rights that prisoners have but is styled to help diminish the level of complexity that impedes the rights of everybody. Lowering the level of difficulty can provide for accelerating the whole process of getting potentially eligible candidates for an exit moving out faster and or better equipped to succeed.

There is a phrase about consequential damages to the whole incarceration experience that is further complicated by delays. Delays can lead to stress and tension within the facility, and that can stifle hope and positivity.

The inability of prisoners to see exit options may have kept the pressure in prison at a dangerous level. In segmentation, that level of intensity may be split and more manageable for all so that they can begin to see new options from prior circumstances.

As prisoners age, their threat to the community can drop as can their flexibility and ability to take care of themselves. The threat assessment, medical assessment, and any disability determination can all be indicators of a reduction in their ability to be a threat to the community.

Prisoners who are no longer a physical threat could be released if we initiate a systematic method of making that determination. A system like that could enhance many lives and save the taxpayers many dollars.

A system like that would not have to be a new expense to the prison because the facility already has the responsibility to care for the prisoners. A few administrative changes with a prisoner's privacy waiver might make it a no-cost game changer.

# 14 - Self Aware and Nation Serving

You can do an excellent service for yourself, the prison system and the nation by maximizing every opportunity to determine your future situation. While it may seem to be too late and make no sense to put forth the effort, I invite you to reassess everything in light of the reality of your situation now.

Regardless of what has gone before, there is a congruency of a personal reality check that can give you a perspective and motivation toward a new situation that you previously may not have seen as possible.

Like many things in life, you can change when circumstances, people, events, and motivations shift. Your aging self can be quite a paradoxical dynamo when you understand your options.

You may have a bucket list, and it may seem impossible. When I do pastoral rounds at a local hospital, I see a lot of the effects of conditioned thinking.

Conditioned thinking is the result of taking your experience and using it as a filter upon which you see all that is possible in the world. While that process may be a familiar perspective for you to project the future naturally, it has a limitation in that there is no possibility to introduce anything that is new and fresh and different.

Conditioned thinking does not motivate and empower, it only limits. You may think you need to worry and surrender. Not a great idea when you could reevaluate and create a B plan that could work.

You may be too young to cave into pessimism. Why not, play with new ideas.

You are where you are, and you have some future, or you would have been gone already. Nobody knows why they have come to planet earth or precisely what they are supposed to do while they are here.

Segmentation may offer you a whole new set of options that you could have never imagined previously. Age may have changed you in many ways, and that may allow you some unique opportunities.

It will likely be a massive challenge for you to understand all that could be because some conditioned thinking may still limit your vision. That could change if segmentation brings you more peace and your view of possibility shifts.

I would encourage you to use your time to reinvestigate all the potentials of your life that are untapped.

Also, please investigate options for your release from prison through Compassionate release programs.

Earlier in 2017, the U.S. Senate Appropriations Committee addressed the concerns that Families Against Mandatory Minimums (FAMM) raised about the Bureau of Prisons lack of activity to increase the use of a compassionate release.

They requested the releases granted and denied and the reason for those decisions within the last five years.

# 15 - Angel Raphael Light

Before the Angel invitation referenced in the Introduction above, Angel Raphael embraced the prison pessimism that so permeates the energy of the thinking and disconnection in prison.

Subtle but important is the distinction of why I use Angel Raphael Speaks when Angel Raphael is a powerhouse. Archangel Raphael Speaks felt very cumbersome and off-putting to me, so there was a lot of back and forth about the title. This, by the way, was before Angel Raphael sent the first message about prison which was message eight and surprised me.

## "Prison Life of the Future

The complexity of your prison systems is detrimental to many that occupy, serve, visit, and guard them. There is a palpable intensity of negativity present at most facilities.

When one can change their mind, they can improve their reality. Could it be that your society could realign prison life to contain the expansion of the need for more prisons?

Unions should not worry as there is no suggestion that these places can be eliminated any time in upcoming centuries. Union leaders could help serve their members by helping the institutions become more user-friendly and economical for all.

The word economical was included to get the attention of the administrators, but the goal is really to promote the lessening of dehumanization that exists within the societal dynamics from which the crop of criminals grows. The guard and others who work for institutions are exposed to the negative energy of the collected criminals, and that is not exactly a nurturing vibration.

Please consider as if the vibration of a prison existed on a scale that you could read called the love fear continuum. Consider that a single increment move on that scale that went away from fear and moved towards love was actually beneficial to all who passed through the premises.

As you ever so slightly held that thought, you entertained the possibility of a shift for the imprisoned and guards of the future. Congratulations, for you, have allowed some light to shine on a subject that is almost perpetually locked in pessimism." ARS 9

Please feel free to talk to the Angels and find your Peace.
Blessed Be AND SO IT IS!

Three Powerful Angels
Archangel Michael - Protection
Archangel Raphael - Healing
Archangel Gabriel - Communication

# 16 - Thank You

# For Considering These Ideas

# 17 - Don't Worry Ever

# Ever

# It Does Not Help Prayer Still Does!

Resource: http://www.Create-A-Prayer.com

# 18 - Resource Books

Distant Healing Sessions (or Join Mail List) – Write To mikewann@voicenet.com

## Books by Rev. Mike at www.Amazon.com

Veterans Healing Six Pack
1. *Trauma Healing Options for VA Hospitals: Help for Veterans to Own Their Healing and their future.*
2. *Trauma Healing Action Steps for Veterans: Help to Start Healing*
3. *Trauma Healing Action Steps for Veterans: Empowerment*
4. *Trauma Healing Action Steps for Veterans: Forgiveness*
5. *Trauma Healing Action Steps for Veterans: Thought Freedom*
6. *Tea For Veterans: Welcome One Home*

PTSD Power Pack:
1. *The PTSD Project: Turn Pain To Power*
2. *PTSD & Soul Retrieval: Putting One Back Together*
3. *PTSD & The Purple PAD: Calling all Scientists and PTSD Patients*

*Angel Raphael Speaks Volume 1: Take Courage! God Has Healing in Store for You!*
*Angel Raphael Speaks Volume 2: Take Courage! God Has Healing in Store for You!*
*Angel Raphael Speaks Volume 3: Take Courage! God Has Healing in Store for You!*
*Angel Raphael Speaks Volume 4: Angels, Addicts, Alcoholics & Prisoners – Oh Yeah!*
*Angel Raphael Speaks Volume 5:* Prisoners Caring for Alcoholics - Australia In Miniature Projects Intro
*Angel Raphael Speaks Volume 6:* Prisoners Caring for Addicts - Australia In Miniature For Addicts
*Reiki Journaling from Japan*
*Reiki Is Alive: God's Great Gift*
*Four Parts to Healing*
*Distant Healing: We Are All Connected*
*Stress Release Energy Work: How To Cope*
*Does Reiki Love Heal Cancer?*
*Group Consciousness*
*Salute To Philadelphia VA Medical Center: Thank You*
*Reiki Transcript for Reiki 2 & 3 Channels: Dr. Usui Is That You?*
*God Bless Kindle & Amazon*
*Puppies Are Different From People*
*If Your Dog Dies*
*Toy Guns Are Obsolete*

*Great Spirit Made Children With Red Skin: AND*
*The Cage of Fear: Is Not Locked*
*God Made Children Red, Yellow, Brown, Black & White: Greet Each Child With Kindness*
*Emergency Medical Kindness In The Cradle Of Liberty: Big City - Cracked Bell*
*Angels Are Always Around Addicts and Addicts: Help Is Near Now! Invite It In!*
*Angels Are Always Around Addicts and Alcoholics: Volume 2 - Tools To Help Re-Light...*
*Prison Jobs Now: Providing Care For Addicts And Addicts*
*Controlled Care Communities Concept*
*Prison Possibilities Dialogue Series: Concept*
*Prison Possibilities Dialogue Series: Volume 2, 3, 4, 5 Dialogues*
*Prison Possibilities Voluntary Exile*
*Prison Possibilities Corrections Coaches*
*Prison Possibilities For Mexicans: Is A Boat Better Than A Wall?*
*Prison Possibilities Family Time:* A Reason to Thrive!
Prison Genius Pool: "So Much Genius In Jail."
*Prison Possibilities Access Control: Prisoner Access by Request*
*Prisoner's Lawyers Can Save The American Economy: Make A Buck Doing It & ...*
*Prisoner Family Talks, Days, Stays & Vacations: Connecting Helps Healing*
*Prisoner Writing Projects: Write To Heal, Start Over & Reconnect*
*Prison Cell Clearing & Blessing: Clear Entities, Chase Ghosts, & Create Sacred Space*
*Prisoner Professors: Show You Are Aware Create Change With Care*
*Prison Reiki? Maybe Someday? A Gateway To Help Heal Prisons & America?*
*Judges and An Angel Rule On Possibilities: We Can Cut Sentences & Prison Costs*
*Ideas For Prison Wardens: Leadership Is Not Easy*
*Solitary Community: Could Community Support Cut Costs and Issues?*
*Prison Project Communications Team: Communications Can Change Lives*
*Motivating & Empowering Prisoners? Invite Prisoners To Find Their Motivation*
*Prison Segmentation For Safety, And Sanity, Security, Peace, and Space*
*Prison Segmentation For Security*
*Dowsing for Prisoners; Answers from Above*
Ex-Prisoner Possibilities With Real Estate Investors
*Prison Segmentation For Joint Ventures*
*Prison Segmentation For Your Rehabilitation: R U Ready?*
*Prison Segmentation For Family Villages*

Little Books at Kindle.com by Rev. Mike:
*English Medical History Questionnaire For Non-English Speakers*
*English Language Helper For Non-English Speakers*
*Wise Wonderful Women Are The Well Of The Family*
*Answers for Test & Research: Dowsing Power*
*Crisis? Reiki! Baby? Reiki!*
*Bible References For Healing*
*Angel Raphael Speaks – Prisons*
*Angel Raphael Speaks – Veterans*
*The Saint Off Interstate 95*

# 19 - Angels Please Prayers

**Addict's**

Angels of Healing Selected
Help Me to Stay Directed
Come To Me From The Sky
I Am Ready to Succeed Not Try
If I Don't Invite You In
I Might Not Win
I Have Been Lost For Too Long
Help Me To Stay Strong

**Alcoholic's**

Angels of Healing On High
Help Me to Stay Dry
Come To Me From The Sky
I Am Ready to Succeed Not Try
If I Don't Invite You In
I Might Not Win
I Have Been Lost For Too Long
Help Me To Stay Strong

# From

http://AngelRaphaelSpeaks.com/AAAAAA/

# 20 - Private Channeling

Angel Raphael Speaks a series of free messages that are channeled through Reverend Mike Wanner for the Highest good and Highest Healing of all concerned.

Many questions arise about Reverend Mike doing private channeling, and he does help with that so e-mail him.

Reverend Mike is available worldwide as a psychic channel, emotional release facilitator, spiritual energy practitioner & teacher, and public speaker. He looks forward to meeting you soon!

Email - mikewann@voicenet.com 215-342-1270 PRIVATE SPIRITUAL READINGS/channelings or Spiritual Healing Sessions: Telephone or in person. Rev. Mike is available for private, one-on-one intuitive sessions with you, his Guide Family, and your Guides. He helps by offering clarity on emotional situations about your life, your purpose, your spirituality, and the release of stuffed emotions and cellular memory.
Connect to the love of your Guides today!
Contact Rev. Mike for an appointment.

Sessions available:

Spiritual Readings
Angel Channeling
Distant Reiki Healing
Remote Clearing of Stuffed Emotions
Distant Clearing Cellular Memory
Distant Clearing Energy Blockages
Remote Clearing of the Chakras
Customized needs
Mastermind dowsing responses to yes/no direction finding questions.

Rev. Mike is a facilitator of healing. He brings you and the Divine together so that you can align with the Divine and have a great time and a great life. All healing is between you and God, as it should be. Go ahead and start without Rev. Mike. Visit his prayer site http://www.Create-A-Prayer.com. Take the first step NOW.

# 21 - Reverend Mike Wanner

Rev. Mike Wanner started his Metaphysical and Ministerial studies with Reiki in 1993 and had studied seven styles of Reiki in the U.S., Japan, Canada, Denmark and Australia. He is certified to teach. He became certified to teach Integrated Energy Therapy in 1999 and co-taught the first IET class of the new Millennium. Mike began dowsing in 2001.

Ordained as a Metaphysical Minister of the International Metaphysical Ministry and an Interfaith Minister of the Circle of Miracles Ministry, Rev. Mike practices and teaches spiritual energy therapies in the Philadelphia Area.

Rev. Mike holds ministerial degrees from the University of Metaphysics and the University of Sedona. He is a Pastoral Care Associate at Aria - Frankford Hospital. He taught at the National Academy of Massage Therapy and Health Sciences.

Rev. Mike was a faculty member of the Medical Mission Sister's Center for Human Integration's School of Integrated Body/Mind Therapies in Fox Chase, Philadelphia, PA for twelve years.

Rev. Mike is licensed by the teaching of Intuitional Metaphysics to practice Spiritual Healing and Scientific Prayer. Mike is also a Prayer therapist.

Rev. Mike was elected in 2007 to the status of "Fellow of the American Institute of Stress."

In 2008, Rev. Mike became a practitioner of Coincidental Recognition as he incorporated the CoRe System into his spiritual healing practice.

In 2009, Rev. Mike trademarked a new healing process called Quantum Quatro! Subtle Energy System Support®.

In 2011, Rev. Mike joined the outreach program known as the Health Advantage Group.

In 2012, Rev. Mike became a Certified Professional Coach by The Master Coaching Academy and Joined the Personal Empowerment Group.

Before his Metaphysical, Ministerial and Coaching studies, Rev. Mike worked for Sears Roebuck and Co. while in High School and after graduation, until he joined the U. S. Air Force in 1965. He returned to Sears from Vietnam in 1969 and stayed until 1978. His final Sears assignment was as an efficiency expert in Methods - Operational Research and Development.

He volunteered with Burholme Emergency Medical Services from 1969 and is still a Life Member and Board of Directors Member. He started a private ambulance company in 1975 and worked professionally in the field until 2001 when he devoted his full attention to real estate investing, healing, coaching, and writing.

# May All Who Read This Be Blessed AND SO IT IS!

www.ingramcontent.com/pod-product-compliance
Lightning Source LLC
Chambersburg PA
CBHW050035230526
45470CB00003B/1297